Invocations

Also by Richard Skinner

Leaping & Staggering (Dilettante, 1988;1996)
In the Stillness: a sequence of poems based on Julian of Norwich
(Dilettante, 1990)
The Melting Woman (Blue Button, 1993)
Still Staggering … (Dilettante, 1995)
Echoes of Eckhart (Arthur James, 1998)
The Logic of Whistling (Cairns, 2002)

Invocations

Calling on the God in All

Richard Skinner

WILD GOOSE PUBLICATIONS

Copyright © Richard Skinner, 2005

Published by
Wild Goose Publications
4th Floor, Savoy House, 140 Sauchiehall St, Glasgow G2 3DH, UK
web: www.ionabooks.com
Wild Goose Publications is the publishing division of the Iona
Community. Scottish Charity No. SCO03794. Limited Company
Reg. No. SCO96243.

ISBN 1 901557 93 6

Cover illustration © Inkadinkado, Inc. Designed by Virginia Wadland
www.inkadinkado.com

A catalogue record for this book is available from the British Library.

Overseas distribution
Australia: Willow Connection Pty Ltd, Unit 4A, 3-9 Kenneth Road,
Manly Vale, NSW 2093
New Zealand: Pleroma, Higginson Street, Otane 4170,
Central Hawkes Bay
Canada: Bayard, 49 Front Street East, Toronto, Ontario M5E 1B3

Permission to reproduce any part of this work in Australia or New
Zealand should be sought from Willow Connection.

Produced by Reliance Production Company, Hong Kong
Printed and bound in China

for Elizabeth

INTRODUCTION

I was inspired to develop the following forty invocations having for several years much appreciated Jim Cotter's *Cries of Advent* (Cairns Publications, 1989), a series of meditations for the first 24 days of December. The *Cries* in their turn spring from the 'Advent Antiphons' which are best known through their incorporation in the Christian hymn *O Come, O Come Emmanuel*.

An antiphon is a short liturgical chant sung responsively by two choirs. The Advent Antiphons, usually attributed to Pope Gregory the Great, are known as 'the Great "O"s'. Each one addresses Christ with a title derived from the Old Testament, such as 'O Key of David', 'O Adonai', 'O Dayspring'. This title is then briefly amplified before the antiphon concludes with a petition, e.g.: '*O Adonai, Ruler of the House of Israel; you appeared to Moses in the fire of the burning bush, and gave him the law on Mount Sinai; Come, redeem us with your outstretched arm.*'

My invocations differ somewhat from this structure in that the opening address or invocation is directed more to that which is providing the image (*O Earthworm, O Pearl, O Shout of Laughter*) than specifically to Christ or God (or the Godhead, or the Divine, or the Transcendent, or whichever inadequate term, if any, one might have in mind). The concluding petition, however, is addressed to that particular aspect of God (or the Godhead, or the Divine …) for which the opening image now becomes a metaphor. The hinge between the two parts of each invocation is its sixth line, beginning *You are…*, which simultaneously refers back to the opening image and forward to the concluding petition.

I have also deliberately not drawn upon symbolism either from the Bible or from other sacred writings for any of the opening images (which in some instances is pretty obvious: neither CD-ROMs nor DNA get much of a mention in any religious or spiritual tradition I know of), but rather from creation, science, technology and human psychology. However, in the main body of some of the invocations, Christian iconography is alluded to as that is my background and the language I am most familiar with. My hope though is that these invocations will be used by individuals, groups and gatherings of any or no religious or spiritual allegiance.

O Dragonfly

gauze-winged creature of the air,

gracile dart of downy emerald;

rising high above your pond-bug incarnation

whose husk is clasping the reed;

you are the metamorphosis:

come, free us from our old constraints,

send us winging into risen life.

O Moth

frail frame borne

on wings of patterned dust,

battering at the window of night,

insistent for the light within;

you are the pattern for persistence:

come, batter at our intransigence,

we who seek to shut you out.

O Jackdaw

bold and bright-eyed,

collector of gleam and glitter,

purloiner of jewels that wink and shine,

gleaner of litter that glistens;

you are the gatherer of all that delights:

come, cast your eyes upon us,

catch beneath its tarnish the sparkle of our soul.

O Earthworm

toiling in darkness, ingesting the soil,

fashioning the bronchioles

through which the earth breathes,

signing your work with coiled humility;

you are significance beneath the surface:

come, tunnel in our darkness, bring breath,

mark us with your signature.

O Dung Beetle

forager in filth,

waste-user, detritus-devourer,

cleanser of ordure and all that befouls,

your body the chamber of change;

you are the purification:

come, forage in the dung of our decisions,

transmute the harmful and hurtful.

O Starfish

pentagram of the deep,

singular descendant from the night sky;

beached by the sea's long retreat,

sprawled among junk and bladder-wrack;

you are two realms united by one name:

come, return to our troubled depths,

reunite us with the glory of the heavens.

O Seahorse

curled into an ocean's interrogative,

concealed in sinuous weed,

paternal pouch proud

with vibrant young;

you are the all-providing father who mothers:

come, entrust us to the ocean swell,

we who give birth to our own questionings.

O Emperor Penguin

comically waddling across the vast ice,

hesitant before the clumsy plunge,

gliding in the glacial depths

with a wondrous gracefulness;

you are the subverter of expectation:

come, surprise us in our hesitations,

plunge us into grace.

O Ammonite

offspring of the ages,

captured and compressed in the rock,

at one with the rock,

revealed now by the splitting of the rock;

you are the teacher of the mystery of our origins:

come, show us our beginning and our end

in the one Rock.

O Mountain Spring

fresh and clear,

speaking of a hidden source,

seeping to a rill, a stream, a river,

hinting of a distant sea;

you are our journey's alpha:

come, refresh us as we travel on towards

the ocean's omega.

O Thunderous Ocean

mighty, immeasurable,

relentless bombardment of the land,

hollowing out caves, wearing down cliffs,

flinging up fragments of fleeting rainbow;

you are power ever-present:

come, undermine the resistance of our unbelief,

erode the reluctance of our doubt.

O Lichen

coloniser of unpromising places,
patchworking old walls and rocky outcrops
with sombre stains,
embossing bark and rotten stumps;
you are the vanguard of new growth:
come, colonise every crevice of our heart,
stain us with intimations of your presence.

O Leaf

receptor of the sun,

powerhouse of the tree;

withering and dying at the year's end,

falling to feed the roots anew;

you are the round of life with death:

come, take us through death to life

by the tree on which you hang.

O Thorn

protector of the rose,

wounding unwary fingers that would pluck the rose;

embedded in flesh,

warning of the frailty of flesh;

you are mortality's envoy:

come, prick our conscience, wound our vanity,

protect us from the envoys of evil.

O Pinecone

clenched fist of the forest,

knuckled custodian of the maturing seed,

at the season's signal releasing the captive

to the caprice of the wind;

you are the security of letting go:

come, at the season of our dispersal,

scatter us in the freedom of the Spirit.

O Hedgerow

erratic weave of shrub and bramble

where small creatures burrow through leaf-mould;

line of sportive wood dividing fields,

enclosing flock, protecting crop;

you are boundary, you are barrier:

come, at the hostile hour,

absorb the storm, confound the predator.

O FOREST FIRE

intense and uncontainable,

engulfing all that cannot flee the flame,

assuming the living and the dead

into your own being;

you are the consummation:

come, rage through us, consume us,

we who would be of one nature with you.

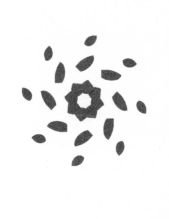

O FROST

transfiguring fields overnight

to silent stillness,

sealing in the land's abundance

beneath your cold carapace;

you are the time of endurance in hardship:

come, endure with us now,

shelter the promise of spring.

O Blizzard

swift and terrible,

blotting out the world,

obliterating all distinction, all separate identity,

with a whiteness of blinding brilliance;

you are ferocity in softness:

come, blot out our every fault and failing,

overwhelm us with your generosity.

O Storm Cloud

siege-engine of the sky,

rumbling into place to assault the dry earth;

amorphous menace,

unleashing, spending, pouring down your fullness;

you are self-emptying made manifest:

come, besiege our arid understanding,

pour your riches into the poverty of our thought.

O Shaft of Lightning

blasting an ancient beech,

toppling a proud steeple,

tearing apart at a stroke

the very fabric of the air;

you are dazzle and destruction from on high:

come, shock us with your vehemence,

strike at our constructions of ignorance.

O Darkness

as potent as a curse,

as fragile as a candle flame,

as threatening as a foe,

as comforting as a friend;

you are the womb for all qualities:

come, endow us with your fecundity,

enrich us with your every paradox.

O Stars

diamond dust
strewn across the velvet heaven,
uncountable points of fire
fusing atom with atom with atom;
you are the crucible of creation:
come, forge our dust into spirit
in the alchemical fire of your love.

O Comet

glowing sky-smudge heading sunwards,

hair flowing in the solar wind;

swinging round, speeding back to distant dark,

turning to return in distant time;

you are glory, transient but recurrent:

come, glow, blaze your trail

across our humdrum days.

O Pearl

secretly accreting in the oyster shell,

your nacreous layers around the irritant heart;

O tiny sphere of cool,

condensed light;

you are affliction made precious:

come, enclose the grit of our doubt in hope,

that we might shine with your beauty.

O Oil

phial of aromatic purity,

crushed and distilled from herb and flower

to ease the aching body,

to anoint at death's transition;

you are healing, you are unction:

come, spilt for our benefit,

ease the minds of all who are troubled.

O Salt

fierce metal married to poison gas,

generating the taste of tears,

gratifying the lick of the wild beast,

eliciting the full flavour of the feast;

you are the universal seasoning:

come, marry your fierce love to our hurts

that we may savour you.

O Speck of Dust

caught in a shaft of sunlight

dancing along a random pathway,

jostled by unseeable molecules,

swirled by momentary currents;

you are the interplay of chance and necessity:

come, jostle us from the path of complacency,

join us in the unpredictable dance.

O Bell

massive swung metal, hung high,

sounding, resounding, giving tongue to one cry,

full-throated with one vowel

for which you were formed;

you are invitation and calling:

come, sound out loud again and clear

for all who feign deafness.

O Garden Fork

soil-turner, weed-uprooter,

clod-breaker, compost-spreader;

O simple tool shaped

for such simple use;

you are the task and the toil:

come, till the wastelands within us,

prepare our unproductive ground

to receive the seed.

O CD-ROM

information's halo,
where image, sound and word
await their resurrection
at the touch of a laser;
you are the unknown made known:
come, transcending image, sound, word,
inform our waiting clay.

O Electron

charged with the duty of atomic handshakes,

creator of an atom's activity,

ever-obedient to the laws that govern

your particular orbit;

you are the fulfilment of that which you are:

come, charge our every activity

with obedience to that which we are.

O DNA

spring of life, coiled for life,

cell-centre's delicate thread

untwisting, re-twisting,

spiralling down through generations;

you are the code of our being:

come, coil in our soul-centre,

transcribe yourself in the nucleus of our will.

O Absolute Zero

absolute rest,

absolute absence of anything;

always approachable, never attainable,

at the limit of infinite steps;

you are the cessation of all striving:

come, overleap the absolute limit,

that restless hearts may rest in you.

O Circle

O perfect form, ideal form,

no beginning and no end;

encompassing every direction,

subsuming every symmetry;

you are centre and circumference:

come, draw us into your round,

form us into your perfection.

O Shout of Laughter

outburst of indecorous noise,

explosion of absurdity,

shaking the helpless body with glee,

puncturing the proud and the pompous;

you are the destroyer of convention:

come, upend our tables of pomposity and pride

with your sudden detonations.

O DOUBT

offspring of knowledge,

shadow-side of certainty;

O challenger of comfortable illusion,

interrogator of the well-accepted;

you are the scalpel of the spirit:

come, cut through our layers of self-deception,

excise the errors of blind belief.

O DREAM

royal road to the oracle,

speaker in tongues of sign and symbol;

unscripted drama of the night

where Wisdom plays every part;

you are the vision within:

come, as we close our bodily eyes,

fling wide the doors of inner perception.

O Labyrinth

leading in to the fearsome beast,

leading out to the changeful world;

who will tread your unfamiliar ways?

who will track your convolutions?

you are exploration and destination;

come, embolden us, we who cross your threshold,

lead us to the beast's befriending.

O Poem

words working in concert,

abundance compressed to a single utterance;

articulating the emotion,

capturing the idea and releasing the real;

you are truth in ambiguity:

come, work your words in us,

utter yourself and we shall be.

NOTES

O **Dragonfly:** The 'downy emerald', one of several metallic-green dragonflies, is so-called because it has dense yellow hair on the thorax.

O **Jackdaw:** 'The sparkle of our soul' alludes to the imagery used by, among others, the mystic Meister Eckhart who frequently referred to the indwelling of God as the 'spark of the soul'.

O **Seahorse:** In this remarkable species, the male has the responsibility for nurturing the young as soon as they are conceived, so he, in effect, subsequently gives birth to them.

O **Hedgerow:** In *Lines composed a few miles above Tintern Abbey,* William Wordsworth describes hedgerows as 'little lines of sportive wood run wild'.

O **Speck of Dust:** *Chance and Necessity* is the title of a book by the scientist Jacques Monod.

O **Electron:** The structure of the outer electron shell of an atom determines its ability to form bonds with other atoms.

O Absolute Zero: Absolute zero (-273.15°C) is the temperature at which a physical system has the lowest possible energy. According to the third law of thermodynamics, it can never be achieved, only approached as the limit of an infinite number of steps. The last line cribs St Augustine's assertion that 'our hearts are restless till they find their rest in Thee'.

O Circle: St Augustine again, who defined the nature of God as 'a circle whose centre is everywhere and circumference nowhere'.

O Doubt: Doubt as the 'offspring of knowledge' is cribbed from *The Martyrdom of Man* by Winwood Reade.

O Dream: Sigmund Freud, founder of psychoanalysis, referred to dreams as 'the royal road to the Unconscious'; and the poet William Blake writes that 'if the doors of perception were cleansed, everything would appear to man as it is, infinite'. Aldous Huxley borrowed the image for a book title, and a 60s' rock group shortened it to *The Doors*.

Wild Goose Publications, the publishing house of the Iona Community established in the Celtic Christian tradition of St Columba, produces books, tapes and CDs on:

- holistic spirituality
- social justice
- political and peace issues
- healing
- innovative approaches to worship
- song in worship, including the work of the Wild Goose Resource Group
- material for meditation and reflection

If you would like to find out more about our books, tapes and CDs, please contact us at:

Wild Goose Publications
Fourth Floor, Savoy House
140 Sauchiehall Street,
Glasgow G2 3DH, UK

Tel. +44 (0)141 332 6292
Fax +44 (0)141 332 1090
e-mail: admin@ionabooks.com

or visit our website at
www.ionabooks.com
for details of all our products and online sales